THE AUSTRALIAN
Women's Weekly
food for kids
with allergies

BAUER

MEDIA GROUP

CONTENTS

coping with allergies: you're not alone

If you have just learned that your child has a food allergy, take comfort from the knowledge that you are not alone. Food allergies now affect 10% of children under the age of one, and 4-8% of children under five years. It might be a mild allergy, which causes eczema, vomiting or upset bowels, and there is a good chance that this allergy will disappear in a couple of years. Or it might be severe, which is every parent's nightmare. A particle of food the size of a grain of sand could trigger a massive response causing anaphylaxis and threatening your child's life. Your life will never be the same. How do you keep your child safe? What can you do? Here are some tips and guidelines that other parents have found to be useful.

Always ensure that your child has the appropriate medication to treat their allergic reaction with them at all times. If possible, do not have the food to which your child is allergic (the food allergen) in your house. For example, if your child has a peanut allergy, do not have peanut butter in the cupboard. Some food allergens are difficult to avoid in a normal household, such as milk, wheat and eggs. If these foods are necessary in your kitchen, ensure they are kept well away from other foods that your child will eat, perhaps in a specially marked area.

If you take your child to visit friends or relatives, tell them about your child's food allergy in advance. Many people are sceptical or do not understand how dangerous a food allergy can be, so you may have to outline what could happen if your child does ingest the food allergen. If your child is having a 'sleepover', be sure to explain to the parents how to use the medication.

Always carry safe food with you and, if going to a child's party, provide extra safe food to share so that your child does not feel too different.

After preparing foods that contain the food allergen, always wash hands, cooking pots, pans and utensils well to remove all traces. A quick rinse under the cold tap is not enough.

If you are going to a restaurant, tell the waiter/waitress that your child has a food allergy. Better still, telephone before going and ask to speak with the chef.

When choosing a pre-school or childcare centre, select a facility that is food allergy-aware. You may prefer that your child attend a school that does not allow a particular food allergen. Ask questions such as: Are children allowed to bring (your child's food allergen)? And, if so, what safeguards are in place to ensure that your child will not come into contact with that food? Check that teachers or carers have been educated in the treatment of allergic reactions, particularly if adrenalin injections (EpiPens or Anapens) are needed.

When travelling on any form of transport where food is provided, such as an airline, alert the carrier that your child has a food allergy and pack safe food to take with you just in case.

In Australia, labelling of food allergens on packaged foods is law. All the major allergens – dairy, wheat, egg, soy, peanuts, sesame, tree nuts, fish, shellfish – must be identified on the label. This means that a manufacturer is breaking the law if one of these foods is present and is not identified on the label. Be aware of all the different names used for the food your child must avoid. Always read food labels, even if you have bought the food before and it was previously safe. When buying food that is not packaged, the vendor (seller) is required by law to tell you the ingredients of the food or meals, if asked. Unfortunately, in practice, this is difficult because the vendor is not necessarily the person who prepared the food. The vendor may not know all of the ingredients and may not be aware of possible contamination of the food with food allergens. For example, a homemade cake bought at a school fair is not labelled and you could expect it to contain egg, wheat and milk. However, it might be contaminated with peanut because the generous mother who made the cake was also cooking peanut biscuits at the same time. If in doubt, it is always best to be cautious.

With all these restrictions it is common for children to feel that they are 'different', and we all know how hard this can be. We are fortunate in that food manufacturers over the past few decades have developed many alternative products to those containing food allergens, but this does not always help the child who just wants to be like their friends. By preparing meals that the whole family can enjoy you will be helping your child to understand that they can still eat 'normally'.

In this book you will find recipes for tasty, normal foods and meals that are naturally free of the major food allergens or have been modified to replace one or more food allergens. I hope your children and your whole family will enjoy these delicious, low allergy recipes.

Linda Hodge
Accredited Practising Dietitian
B.Sc. M.Sc. (Med.) A.P.D. A.N.

A gluten-free diet doesn't need to be dull. In fact, now you can bake a cake and your child can eat it too. A gluten-free diet has almost become mainstream – gluten-free flour, baking powder, bread and some great edible cake decorations can be purchased in supermarkets without any hassle.

test kitchen tip

These pancakes make a
great snack; pack them
in the school lunch box
for morning tea.

savoury buckwheat pancakes

PREP + COOK TIME 30 MINUTES **MAKES** 10

1 cup (150g) buckwheat flour

½ cup (60g) gluten-free plain (all-purpose) flour

3 teaspoons gluten-free baking powder

2 eggs

2 cups (500ml) buttermilk

50g (1½ ounces) butter, melted

1 small carrot (70g), grated coarsely

1 medium zucchini (120g), grated coarsely

½ cup (80g) fresh or frozen corn kernels

1 Sift dry ingredients into a large bowl; gradually whisk in the combined eggs and buttermilk until smooth. Stir in melted butter and vegetables.

2 Heat a lightly oiled small frying pan over medium heat, pour ⅓ cup of the batter into pan; cook until bubbles appear on the surface. Turn pancake; cook until browned lightly on the other side. Repeat with remaining batter to make a total of 10 pancakes.

3 Serve pancakes topped with spreadable cream cheese and extra corn kernels, if you like.

nutritional count per pancake
▶ 6.5g total fat
▶ 3.7g saturated fat
▶ 695kJ (166 cal)
▶ 22.1g carbohydrate
▶ 4.1g protein
▶ 0.9g fibre

waffles with maple syrup

PREP + COOK TIME 45 MINUTES **MAKES** 8

You need a waffle iron for this recipe.

200g (6½ ounces) dairy-free spread

¾ cup (165g) caster (superfine) sugar

1 teaspoon vanilla extract

3 eggs, separated

1¼ cups (185g) potato flour

1 cup (160g) brown rice flour

1 teaspoon gluten-free baking powder

1 cup (250ml) water

cooking-oil spray

2 teaspoons pure icing (confectioners') sugar

1 cup (250ml) pure maple syrup

1 Beat spread, caster sugar and extract in a medium bowl with an electric mixer until light and fluffy. Beat in egg yolks one at a time.
2 Beat egg whites in a small bowl with an electric mixer until soft peaks form; gently fold into egg yolk mixture.
3 Fold sifted dry ingredients and the water into egg mixture. (Do not overmix. Mixture may look slightly curdled at this stage.)
4 Spray a heated waffle iron with cooking oil; pour ½ cup batter over the bottom element of the waffle iron. Close iron; cook waffle for about 3 minutes or until browned both sides and crisp. Transfer waffle to a plate; cover to keep warm. Repeat with cooking oil and remaining batter to make a total of 8 waffles.
5 Dust waffles with sifted icing sugar and serve with maple syrup.

nutritional count per waffle
▶ 21.5g total fat
▶ 5.1g saturated fat
▶ 1914kJ (458 cal)
▶ 64.9g carbohydrate
▶ 3.7g protein
▶ 0.2g fibre

GLUTEN FREE WHEAT FREE DAIRY FREE NUT FREE

test kitchen tip

Waffles can be frozen in an airtight container for up to 3 months. Reheat waffles in the oven.

spinach, ham and poached eggs on toast

test kitchen tips

We used gluten-free turkish rolls for this recipe, but any gluten-free bread is fine providing it's nut-free, if that is relevant to your child. Fresh eggs have thicker whites and will hold a neat shape when poaching.

spinach, ham and poached eggs

PREP + COOK TIME 20 MINUTES SERVES 4

4 eggs

4 slices gluten-free nut-free bread (180g)

75g (2½ ounces) baby spinach leaves

150g (4½ ounces) gluten-free shaved ham

1 Half-fill a large frying pan with water; bring to the boil. Break one egg into a small cup or bowl, carefully slide into pan. Repeat with remaining eggs. When all eggs are in the pan, allow water to return to the boil. Cover pan. Turn off heat; stand about 4 minutes or until a light film of egg white sets over yolks.
2 Meanwhile, toast bread. Top each toast slice with spinach and ham.
3 Remove eggs, one at a time, from the pan using a slotted spoon; briefly place spoon on absorbent paper to blot up any poaching liquid. Top ham with eggs.

nutritional count per serving
- ▶ 9.5g total fat
- ▶ 2.6g saturated fat
- ▶ 1371kJ (328 cal)
- ▶ 37.3g carbohydrate
- ▶ 21.5g protein
- ▶ 2.9g fibre

choc-fudge brownies

PREP + COOK TIME 1¼ HOURS MAKES 18

150g (4½ ounces) butter, chopped coarsely

300g (9½ ounces) dark (semi-sweet) chocolate, chopped coarsely

1½ cups (330g) firmly packed brown sugar

3 eggs

¾ cup (75g) ground hazelnuts (see test kitchen tip, page 15)

½ cup (75g) buckwheat flour

½ cup (120g) sour cream

¼ cup (25g) cocoa powder

1 Preheat oven to 180°C/350°F. Grease 19cm x 29cm (7¾-inch x 11¾-inch) slice pan; line base with baking paper, extending paper 5cm (2 inches) over long sides.
2 Melt butter and chocolate in a medium saucepan over low heat. Add sugar; cook, stirring, 2 minutes. Cool mixture 10 minutes.
3 Stir in eggs, then nuts, flour, sour cream and 2 tablespoons of the sifted cocoa. Spread mixture into pan.
4 Bake brownies about 45 minutes. Cool in pan before cutting into squares. Dust with sifted remaining cocoa to serve.

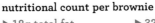

photograph page 14

nutritional count per brownie
- ▶ 18g total fat
- ▶ 9.6g saturated fat
- ▶ 1275kJ (305 cal)
- ▶ 32g carbohydrate
- ▶ 3.6g protein
- ▶ 0.8g fibre

choc-fudge brownies
(recipe page 13)

test kitchen tip

Be aware that some commercially ground hazelnuts, or hazelnut meal, may contain traces of wheat, gluten and peanuts or other nuts. It may be an idea to grind your own using a food processor.

test kitchen tips

Muffins can be stored in the refrigerator in an airtight container for up to 2 days, or frozen for up to 3 months. You can use thinly sliced gluten-free bacon instead of the pancetta, if you like.

pancetta and cheese muffins

PREP + COOK TIME 35 MINUTES **MAKES** 12

1 teaspoon olive oil

200g (6½ ounces) gluten-free pancetta, chopped finely

4 green onions (scallions), sliced thinly

1¼ cups (175g) gluten-free self-raising flour

⅓ cup (55g) polenta

¾ cup (75g) pizza cheese

⅔ cup (160ml) milk

2 eggs

60g (2 ounces) butter, melted

1 Preheat oven to 200°C/400°F. Line a 12-hole (⅓-cup/80ml) muffin pan with paper cases.
2 Heat oil in a medium frying pan over medium-high heat; cook pancetta, stirring, about 3 minutes or until browned lightly. Add onion; cook, stirring, until soft. Cool.
3 Combine flour, polenta and ½ cup of the cheese in a medium bowl; add the combined milk and eggs, melted butter and the pancetta mixture, stir until combined.
4 Divide mixture among paper cases; sprinkle with remaining cheese. Bake about 20 minutes. Stand muffins in pan for 5 minutes before turning, top-side up, onto a wire rack to cool.

nutritional count per muffin
▶ 9.7g total fat
▶ 5.1g saturated fat
▶ 598kJ (143 cal)
▶ 16.7g carbohydrate
▶ 7.2g protein
▶ 0.4g fibre

GLUTEN FREE   WHEAT FREE   NUT FREE

egg, bacon and parmesan pies

PREP + COOK TIME 50 MINUTES (+ REFRIGERATION) **MAKES** 6

2 teaspoons vegetable oil

1 small brown onion (80g), chopped finely

3 gluten-free rindless bacon slices (195g), chopped finely

1 clove garlic, crushed

4 eggs

¼ cup (60ml) pouring cream

¼ cup (20g) finely grated parmesan cheese

1 tablespoon finely chopped fresh chives

GLUTEN-FREE PASTRY

150g (4½ ounces) cold butter, chopped

1 cup (180g) rice flour

¼ cup (35g) (100% corn) cornflour (cornstarch)

¼ cup (30g) soy flour

¼ cup (20g) finely grated parmesan cheese

2 tablespoons cold water, approximately

1 Make gluten-free pastry.

2 Preheat oven to 220°C/425°F. Oil 6-hole ¾-cup (180ml) texas muffin pan.

3 Roll pastry between sheets of baking paper until 5mm (¼-inch) thick; cut six 11cm (4½-inch) rounds from pastry. Ease pastry rounds into pan holes, press into base and sides; prick bases with fork.

4 Bake pastry cases about 10 minutes or until browned lightly. Cool cases in pan. Reduce oven temperature to 200°C/400°F.

5 Heat oil in a small frying pan; cook onion, bacon and garlic, stirring, until bacon is soft. Divide bacon mixture among pastry cases.

6 Whisk eggs and cream in a medium jug; stir in cheese and chives. Fill pastry cases with egg mixture. Bake 25 minutes or until set.

GLUTEN-FREE PASTRY

Process butter, flours and cheese until mixture resembles fine breadcrumbs. Add enough of the water to make ingredients just come together; pulse, then press mixture into a ball. Cover pastry; refrigerate for 30 minutes.

 GLUTEN FREE
 WHEAT FREE
 NUT FREE

18

test kitchen tip

The pies can be stored
in an airtight container
in the fridge for up to
3 days or frozen for
up to 1 month.

nutritional count per pie

▶ 37.9g total fat
▶ 20.8g saturated fat
▶ 2291kJ (548 cal)
▶ 54g carbohydrate
▶ 17.6g protein
▶ 1.5g fibre

test kitchen tips

Cooked polenta fingers
can be stored in an
airtight container in
the refrigerator for
up to 3 days. Polenta
fingers can be eaten
cold, or reheated in the
microwave on HIGH
(100%) for 30 seconds.

zucchini, olive and tomato polenta fingers

PREP + COOK TIME 25 MINUTES (+ REFRIGERATION) **MAKES** 12

2 cups (500ml) water

2 cups (500ml) gluten-free chicken stock

1 cup (170g) polenta

1 large zucchini (150g), grated coarsely

¼ cup (35g) semi-dried tomatoes in oil, drained, chopped finely

½ cup (80g) coarsely chopped seeded black olives

⅓ cup (25g) finely grated parmesan cheese

2 tablespoons olive oil

1 Oil a deep 20cm (8-inch) square cake pan; line base and sides with baking paper.
2 Bring the water and stock to the boil in a large saucepan; gradually stir in polenta. Reduce heat to low; simmer, stirring, about 10 minutes or until polenta thickens.
3 Stir zucchini, tomato, olives and cheese into polenta mixture. Spread mixture into pan; cover, refrigerate about 1 hour or until polenta is firm.
4 Turn polenta onto board; cut in half. Cut each half into six slices.
5 Heat oil in a large frying pan over medium-high heat; cook polenta until browned both sides.

nutritional count per finger
▶ 4.5g total fat
▶ 1g saturated fat
▶ 439kJ (105 cal)
▶ 12.7g carbohydrate
▶ 2.9g protein
▶ 1.1g fibre

potato scones

PREP + COOK TIME 40 MINUTES **MAKES** 12

125g (4 ounces) butter, softened

⅓ cup (55g) pure icing (confectioners') sugar

2 egg yolks

1 cup (230g) sieved cold cooked mashed potato

2 cups (270g) gluten-free self-raising flour

2 teaspoons gluten-free baking powder

2 teaspoons milk, approximately

¼ cup (80g) raspberry jam

¼ cup (60ml) double thick cream

1 Preheat oven to 220°C/400°F. Grease an oven tray.

2 Beat butter, sifted icing sugar and egg yolks in a small bowl with an electric mixer until light and fluffy. Transfer to a large bowl; stir in the mashed potato.

3 Stir sifted flour and baking powder into the potato mixture; mix to a soft dough. Knead dough lightly on a floured surface until smooth.

4 Press dough out into an even 2.5cm (1-inch) thickness. Dip a 5cm (2-inch) round cutter into flour; cut as many rounds as possible from the dough. Place scones 3cm (1¼ inches) apart on oven tray. Gently knead dough scraps together; repeat process to make more scones.

5 Brush tops of scones with milk; bake for 25 minutes or until scones sound hollow when tapped firmly on the top.

6 Serve with jam and cream.

test kitchen tips

You need to cook 2 medium potatoes (380g) for this recipe. The scones are best made and eaten on the same day. They can be frozen for up to 3 months. Thaw in oven, wrapped in foil.

nutritional count per scone

▶ 11.5g total fat

▶ 7.2g saturated fat

▶ 732kJ (175 cal)

▶ 31.5g carbohydrate

▶ 1.6g protein

▶ 0.8g fibre

beef lasagne

PREP + COOK TIME 1½ HOURS SERVES 6

2 teaspoons olive oil

1 medium brown onion (150g), chopped finely

1 small carrot (70g), chopped finely

1 stick celery (150g), trimmed, chopped finely

1 small zucchini (90g), chopped finely

2 cloves garlic, crushed

600g (1¼ pounds) minced (ground) beef

810g (1½ pounds) canned crushed tomatoes

½ cup (140g) tomato paste

16 x 19cm (7¾-inch) rice paper squares

70g (2½ ounces) gluten-free soy cheese, grated (see test kitchen tip)

2 tablespoons finely chopped fresh chives

WHITE SAUCE

1½ cups (375ml) water

1 cup (250ml) gluten-free soy milk (see test kitchen tip)

2 cloves

1 bay leaf

2 tablespoons dairy-free spread

2 tablespoons (100% corn) cornflour (cornstarch)

100g (3 ounces) gluten-free soy cheese (see test kitchen tip), chopped coarsely

1 Heat oil in a large frying pan over high heat; cook onion, carrot, celery, zucchini and garlic, stirring, until onion is soft. Add beef; cook, stirring, until beef is changed in colour. Add tomatoes and paste; cook, stirring, for 10 minutes or until sauce thickens slightly.

2 Meanwhile, make white sauce.

3 Preheat oven to 180°C/350°F. Oil a deep 10-cup (2.5 litre) rectangular ovenproof dish.

4 Dip 8 rice paper squares, one at a time, into a bowl of warm water until soft; place on a board covered with a clean tea towel. Spread 1½ cups beef mixture over base of dish; top with softened rice paper sheets, then half of the remaining beef mixture and half of the white sauce.

5 Soften the remaining rice paper sheets, place on top of the beef mixture; top with remaining beef mixture and white sauce.

6 Bake lasagne, uncovered, for 40 minutes. Sprinkle with cheese; bake a further 15 minutes or until browned lightly. Stand 10 minutes, sprinkle lasagne with chives before serving.

WHITE SAUCE

Combine the water, milk, cloves and bay leaf in a medium saucepan; bring to the boil. Strain milk mixture into a large heatproof jug; discard solids. Melt spread in the same pan; add cornflour, cook, stirring, for 1 minute. Gradually add the hot milk mixture, stirring constantly, until mixture boils and thickens. Stir in cheese.

GLUTEN FREE   WHEAT FREE   DAIRY FREE   EGG FREE   NUT FREE

test kitchen tips

Always check the labels of
soy products carefully for
unexpected allergens.
Lasagne can be stored in
the refrigerator overnight
or frozen for up to 3 months.

nutritional count per serving
- ▶ 23.5g total fat
- ▶ 5.8g saturated fat
- ▶ 1764kJ (422 cal)
- ▶ 20.8g carbohydrate
- ▶ 30.2g protein
- ▶ 4.6g fibre

nutritional count per wedge
capsicum and fetta pizza
▶ 2.5g total fat
▶ 1.3g saturated fat
▶ 560kJ (134 cal)
▶ 23.8g carbohydrate
▶ 2.7g protein
▶ 1.5g fibre

nutritional count per wedge
ham and pineapple pizza
▶ 2.5g total fat
▶ 1.2g saturated fat
▶ 594kJ (142 cal)
▶ 24.1g carbohydrate
▶ 4.4g protein
▶ 1.5g fibre

capsicum and fetta pizza

ham and pineapple pizza

mini pizza wedges

PREP + COOK TIME 50 MINUTES **MAKES** 36 WEDGES (18 OF EACH PIZZA)

500g (1-pound) packet gluten-free nut-free bread mix

½ cup (140g) tomato paste

2 medium tomatoes (300g), sliced thinly

½ small red onion (50g), sliced thinly

270g (8½-ounce) jar char-grilled capsicum (bell pepper) in oil, drained, chopped coarsely

150g (4½ ounces) soft fetta cheese, crumbled

100g (3 ounces) shaved gluten-free ham, chopped coarsely

440g (14 ounces) canned pineapple pieces, drained

1½ cups (150g) pizza cheese

½ cup (60g) seeded green olives, halved

18 small basil leaves

5 cherry tomatoes (100g), quartered

18 fresh oregano leaves

1 Preheat oven to 220°C/425°F. Oil two 25cm x 35cm (10-inch x 14-inch) swiss roll pans; line bases with baking paper, extending paper 5cm (2 inches) over long sides.

2 Make bread according to packet directions; spread mixture into pans. Bake about 12 minutes or until browned lightly. Remove from oven.

3 Spread paste over bases. Top one pizza base with sliced tomato, onion, capsicum and fetta. Sprinkle ham, pineapple and pizza cheese over remaining pizza base.

4 Bake pizzas for 15 minutes or until cheese melts and bases are crisp. Cut each pizza into 18 wedges. Top each capsicum and fetta pizza wedge with olives and basil leaves. Top each ham and pineapple pizza wedge with a cherry tomato and oregano leaf.

test kitchen tip

There are some great gluten-free wraps and pizza bases available at supermarkets; to save time use these for the pizza base.

nutritional count per serving

▶ 55.6g total fat

▶ 34.4g saturated fat

▶ 3102kJ (742 cal)

▶ 43.1g carbohydrate

▶ 17.3g protein

▶ 3.2g fibre

semi-dried tomato and spinach tarts

PREP + COOK TIME 1¼ HOURS (+ REFRIGERATION) **SERVES** 4

20g butter, melted

⅔ cup (160ml) thickened (heavy) cream

1 tablespoon milk

2 eggs

½ cup (80g) coarsely shredded cooked chicken

¼ cup (35g) drained semi-dried tomatoes, chopped finely

25g (¾ ounce) baby spinach leaves, chopped coarsely

GLUTEN-FREE PASTRY

1 cup (180g) rice flour

¼ cup (35g) (100% corn) cornflour (cornstarch)

¼ cup (30g) soy flour

170g (5½ ounces) cold butter, chopped coarsely

2 tablespoons cold water, approximately

1 Make gluten-free pastry.

2 Preheat oven to 220°C/425°F. Grease 11cm x 34cm (4½-inch x 13½-inch) loose-based fluted flan pan with the melted butter.

3 Roll pastry between sheets of baking paper until 5mm (¼-inch) thick. Ease pastry into pan, press into base and sides; trim edge, prick base with fork.

4 Bake pastry case about 15 minutes or until browned lightly. Remove from oven; cool. Reduce oven temperature to 200°C/400°F.

5 Whisk cream, milk and eggs in a medium jug. Fill pastry case with chicken, tomato and spinach; pour in the egg mixture. Bake tart for 25 minutes or until filling is set.

GLUTEN-FREE PASTRY

Process flours and butter until mixture is crumbly. Add enough of the water to make ingredients just come together. Knead dough lightly on a floured surface until smooth. Cover; refrigerate 30 minutes.

test kitchen tips

We found it necessary to grease the pan well with butter. The tart is best made and eaten warm or cold on the same day; it is not suitable to freeze. The pastry can be made 2 days ahead and refrigerated, or frozen for up to a month.

test kitchen tip

Veal escalopes are thinly sliced veal
steak available plain (uncrumbed)
or crumbed; we use plain escalopes
in this recipe.

veal with lemon and oregano

PREP + COOK TIME 20 MINUTES **SERVES** 4

¼ **cup (80ml) olive oil**

2 **cloves garlic, sliced thinly**

¼ **cup fresh oregano leaves**

8 x 100g **(3-ounce) veal escalopes**

1 **teaspoon finely grated lemon rind**

⅔ **cup (160ml) lemon juice**

2 **teaspoons finely chopped flat-leaf parsley**

1 Heat half the oil in a large frying pan over high heat; cook garlic and oregano, stirring, until garlic is browned lightly and oregano is crisp. Remove with a slotted spoon; drain on absorbent paper.

2 Add remaining oil to pan; cook veal, in batches, until browned both sides. Add rind, juice and parsley to pan; cook 1 minute.

3 Serve veal drizzled with pan juices; sprinkle with garlic and oregano mixture.

serving suggestion Serve with mixed salad leaves, if you like.

nutritional count per serving
▶ 21.3g total fat
▶ 3.4g saturated fat
▶ 1576kJ (377 cal)
▶ 1.3g carbohydrate
▶ 45g protein
▶ 0.4g fibre

 GLUTEN FREE
 WHEAT FREE
 DAIRY FREE
EGG FREE
 NUT FREE

brown rice pilaf

PREP + COOK TIME 1¼ HOURS **SERVES** 4

1 medium kumara (orange sweet potato) (200g), chopped coarsely

cooking-oil spray

1 medium lemon (140g)

1 cup (250ml) salt-reduced gluten-free vegetable stock

2 cups (500ml) water

2 teaspoons olive oil

1 medium brown onion (150g), chopped finely

2 stalks celery (300g), trimmed, sliced thinly

2 cloves garlic, crushed

150g (4½ ounces) button mushrooms, halved

1½ cups (300g) brown medium-grain rice

¾ cup loosely packed flat-leaf parsley leaves, chopped coarsely

1 Preheat oven to 180°C/350°F.

2 Place kumara on a baking-paper-lined oven tray; spray lightly with cooking oil. Roast 25 minutes or until tender.

3 Use a zester to remove two thin strips of rind from the lemon.

4 Meanwhile, bring stock and the water to the boil in a small saucepan. Reduce heat; simmer, covered.

5 Heat oil in a medium saucepan over high heat; cook onion, celery and garlic, stirring, until onion softens. Add mushrooms and rice; cook, stirring, 2 minutes. Add stock, reduce heat; simmer, covered, about 40 minutes or until stock is absorbed and rice is tender. Stir in kumara, rind and parsley. Accompany with lemon wedges to serve, if you like.

nutritional count per serving
▶ 5.1g total fat
▶ 0.8g saturated fat
▶ 1551kJ (371 cal)
▶ 68.7g carbohydrate
▶ 9.1g protein
▶ 6.1g fibre

orange syrup cake

PREP + COOK TIME 1¼ HOURS SERVES 8

185g (6 ounces) butter, softened

1 tablespoon finely grated orange rind

1¼ cups (275g) caster (superfine) sugar

6 eggs

3 cups (360g) ground almonds
(see test kitchen tip)

¾ cup (60g) desiccated coconut

¾ cup (150g) rice flour

1 teaspoon gluten-free baking powder

ORANGE SYRUP

2 large oranges (600g)

⅓ cup (75g) caster (superfine) sugar

¼ cup (60ml) water

1 Preheat oven to 160°C/320°F. Grease a 21cm (8½-inch) baba pan well; dust with rice flour, shake out excess.

2 Beat butter, rind and sugar in a medium bowl with an electric mixer until light and fluffy. Add eggs, one at a time, beating until just combined between additions. (Mixture will curdle at this stage, but will come together later.)

3 Stir in ground almonds, coconut and sifted flour and baking powder; spread mixture into pan. Bake, uncovered, for 1 hour.

4 Make orange syrup.

5 Stand cake in pan for 5 minutes; turn onto a wire rack over tray. Pour hot syrup over hot cake.

ORANGE SYRUP

Using a vegetable peeler, slice rind thinly from oranges (or use a citrus zester, if you like, see page 113); cut rind into thin strips. Squeeze juice from oranges (you need ⅔ cup) into a small saucepan; stir in rind, sugar and the water. Stir over high heat, without boiling, until sugar dissolves; bring to the boil. Reduce heat; simmer, uncovered, without stirring, for 5 minutes.

test kitchen tip

Be aware that some commercially ground almonds, or almond meal, may contain traces of wheat, gluten and peanuts or other nuts. It may be an idea to grind your own using a food processor.

nutritional count per serving
▶ 52.9g total fat
▶ 19.3g saturated fat
▶ 3302kJ (790 cal)
▶ 63.7g carbohydrate
▶ 15.8g protein
▶ 5.5g fibre

test kitchen tip

Cakes can be stored in
an airtight container
for up to 3 days.

nutritional count per serving

▶ 18.9g total fat

▶ 7.5g saturated fat

▶ 1180kJ (282 cal)

▶ 27g carbohydrate

▶ 2.5g protein

▶ 1.1g fibre

mandarin, macadamia and polenta cakes

PREP + COOK TIME 1¼ HOURS (+ COOLING) **MAKES** 24

4 small mandarins (400g)

2 cups (280g) unroasted unsalted macadamias

250g (8 ounces) butter, softened

1 cup (220g) caster (superfine) sugar

3 eggs

1 cup (170g) polenta

1 teaspoon gluten-free baking powder

MANDARIN ICING

1⅓ cups (270g) pure icing (confectioners') sugar

20g (¾ ounce) butter, softened

2 tablespoons mandarin juice, approximately

1 Place whole unpeeled mandarins in a medium saucepan, cover with cold water; bring to the boil. Drain then repeat process twice. Cool mandarins to room temperature.

2 Preheat oven to 180°C/350°F. Line two 12-hole (⅓-cup/80ml) muffin pans with paper cases.

3 Blend or process nuts until finely chopped; place in a small bowl.

4 Halve mandarins; discard seeds. Blend or process mandarins and rind until pulpy.

5 Beat butter and sugar in a small bowl with an electric mixer until light and fluffy. Beat in eggs, one at a time. Transfer mixture to a large bowl; stir in polenta, baking powder, nuts and mandarin pulp. Divide mixture between paper cases.

6 Bake cakes about 25 minutes. Stand in pan for 5 minutes before turning, top-side up, onto a wire rack to cool.

7 Make mandarin icing. Spread cold cakes with mandarin icing.

MANDARIN ICING

Sift icing sugar into a small bowl; stir in butter and enough juice to make icing spreadable.

lemon tarts

PREP + COOK TIME 1¼ HOURS (+ REFRIGERATION) **MAKES 6**

1¼ cups (225g) rice flour

¼ cup (35g) (100% corn) cornflour (cornstarch)

¼ cup (30g) soy flour

⅓ cup (75g) caster (superfine) sugar

150g (4½ ounces) cold butter, chopped coarsely

¼ cup (60ml) cold water, approximately

1 tablespoon pure icing (confectioners') sugar

LEMON FILLING

⅔ cup (170g) mascarpone cheese

2 eggs

¼ cup (40g) pure icing (confectioners') sugar

1 tablespoon finely grated lemon rind

½ cup (125ml) lemon juice

1 Process flours, caster sugar and butter until crumbly; add enough of the water to make ingredients come together. Knead dough gently on a floured surface until smooth.

2 Divide pastry into six portions. Roll one portion at a time between sheets of baking paper until large enough to line pans. Ease pastry into pans, pressing into base and side; trim edges, prick base with a fork. Cover; refrigerate 30 minutes.

3 Meanwhile, preheat oven to 180°C/350°F. Grease 6 x 10cm (4-inch) deep loose-based flan pans.

4 Place pans on an oven tray; cover pastry with baking paper, fill with dried beans or uncooked rice. Bake 15 minutes; remove paper and beans carefully from pastry cases. Bake a further 10 minutes; cool.

5 Reduce oven temperature to 150°C/300°F.

6 Make lemon filling; pour filling equally into pastry cases.

7 Bake tarts for 15 minutes or until almost set; cool. Refrigerate 2 hours before serving dusted with sifted icing sugar.

LEMON FILLING

Whisk mascarpone and eggs together in a large jug until smooth. Add sifted icing sugar, rind and juice; whisk until smooth.

GLUTEN FREE WHEAT FREE NUT FREE

test kitchen tip

Tarts can be stored in
an airtight container in
the refrigerator for up
to 2 days.

nutritional count per serving
- ▶ 39.4g total fat
- ▶ 24.9g saturated fat
- ▶ 2491kJ (596 cal)
- ▶ 53.8g carbohydrate
- ▶ 7.4g protein
- ▶ 1.2g fibre

test kitchen tip

Be aware that some commercially ground almonds, or almond meal, may contain traces of wheat, gluten and peanuts or other nuts. It may be an idea to grind your own, using a food processor.

berry cupcakes

PREP + COOK TIME 45 MINUTES MAKES 12

125g (4 ounces) unsalted butter, softened

2 teaspoons finely grated lemon rind

¾ cup (165g) caster (superfine) sugar

4 eggs

2 cups (240g) ground almonds
(see test kitchen tip)

½ cup (40g) desiccated coconut

½ cup (100g) rice flour

1 teaspoon bicarbonate of soda (baking soda)

1 cup (150g) frozen mixed berries

1 Preheat oven to 180°C/350°F. Grease a 12-hole (⅓-cup/80ml) muffin pan.
2 Beat butter, rind and sugar in a small bowl with an electric mixer until light and fluffy. Beat in eggs, one at a time (mixture will separate at this stage, but will come together later). Transfer mixture to a large bowl. Stir in ground almonds, coconut, sifted flour and soda, then berries. Divide mixture into pan holes.
3 Bake cakes for 25 minutes. Stand cakes in pan 5 minutes before turning, top-side up, onto a wire rack to cool. Dust cakes with desiccated coconut or sifted pure icing (confectioners') sugar before serving, if you like.

nutritional count per cupcake
▶ 24.2g total fat
▶ 9.1g saturated fat
▶ 1404kJ (335 cal)
▶ 22.1g carbohydrate
▶ 7.1g protein
▶ 2.7g fibre

GLUTEN FREE WHEAT FREE

DAIRY FREE!

After looking at these fabulous and fun recipes your children will no longer feel left out because they can't eat dairy. This chapter has a great collection of recipes using fresh fruit and vegetables that will be a welcome alternative to everyday dairy drinks and meals.

corned beef hash with poached eggs

PREP + COOK TIME 20 MINUTES **SERVES** 4

1 small brown onion (80g), chopped finely

1½ medium potatoes (300g), grated coarsely

250g (8 ounces) cooked corned beef, finely shredded

1 tablespoon finely chopped flat-leaf parsley

1 tablespoon plain (all-purpose) flour

1 egg

1 tablespoon vegetable oil

4 eggs, extra

1 Combine onion, potato, beef, parsley, flour and egg in a large bowl; shape hash mixture into 8 patties. Heat oil in a large heavy-based frying pan over medium heat; cook patties, uncovered, until browned both sides and potato is tender.

2 Half-fill a large shallow frying pan with water; bring to the boil. Place 4 oiled egg rings into pan. Break 1 extra egg into a small cup; slide into egg rings; repeat with remaining eggs. Return water to the boil; cover pan, turn off heat, stand about 4 minutes or until a light film of egg white sets over the yolks. Remove eggs, one at a time, using a slotted spoon; place on an absorbent paper-lined saucer to blot poaching liquid. Carefully remove egg rings.

3 Serve corned beef hash topped with eggs.

test kitchen tip

If you have no left-over corned beef, combine a 250g (8-ounce) piece of corned beef with 1 chopped onion, 1 chopped carrot, a bay leaf, 6 black peppercorns, 1 tablespoon cider vinegar and 1 tablespoon brown sugar; add enough water to cover the beef in a large saucepan and simmer, covered for 2 hours or until beef is tender. You can also use corned beef from the deli, but ask if it is gluten-free.

DAIRY FREE

NUT FREE

nutritional count per serving
- ▶ 15.1g total fat
- ▶ 4.3g saturated fat
- ▶ 1124kJ (269 cal)
- ▶ 11.2g carbohydrate
- ▶ 21.5g protein
- ▶ 1.4g fibre

baked beans, bacon, tomato and chives

test kitchen tip

Always check the label of
soy products carefully for
unexpected allergens.

baked beans, bacon, tomato and chives

PREP + COOK TIME 15 MINUTES **SERVES** 4

420g (13½ ounces) canned baked beans in tomato sauce

4 rindless bacon slices (240g), sliced thinly

4 slices (180g) dairy-free, egg-free, nut-free multi-grain bread

2 medium tomatoes (300g), chopped coarsely

1 tablespoon finely chopped fresh chives

1 Preheat grill (broiler).

2 Heat baked beans in a small saucepan over medium heat.

3 Meanwhile, cook bacon in a heated small frying pan over high heat, stirring, until crisp; drain on absorbent paper.

4 Toast bread. Top toast with beans, bacon and tomato; grill about 2 minutes or until hot. Sprinkle with chives.

note You can use your favourite allergy-free bread in this recipe.

pear smoothie

PREP TIME 5 MINUTES **MAKES** 1 LITRE (4 CUPS)

2 medium pears (460g)

2 cups (500ml) gluten-free soy milk (see test kitchen tip, page 46)

1 tablespoon honey

1 Peel and core pears; chop flesh coarsely.

2 Blend or process ingredients until smooth.

photograph page 48

---

nutritional count per serving
- ▶ 10.4g total fat
- ▶ 3.2g saturated fat
- ▶ 1450kJ (347 cal)
- ▶ 34.5g carbohydrate
- ▶ 22g protein
- ▶ 7.4g fibre

nutritional count per 250ml (1 cup)
- ▶ 2.8g total fat
- ▶ 0g saturated fat
- ▶ 589kJ (141 cal)
- ▶ 25.5g carbohydrate
- ▶ 1.9g protein
- ▶ 2.6g fibre

pear smoothie
(recipe page 47)

test kitchen tip

You can use shredded
iceberg lettuce instead
of wombok, if you like.

Sam

vegetable rice paper rolls

PREP TIME 35 MINUTES **MAKES** 18

1 large carrot (180g), grated coarsely

2 stalks celery (300g), trimmed, chopped finely

150g (4½ ounces) wombok (napa cabbage), shredded finely

2 teaspoons gluten-free fish sauce

2 teaspoons light brown sugar

1 tablespoon lemon juice

18 x 17cm (6¾-inch) square rice paper sheets

18 mint leaves

1 Combine carrot, celery, wombok, sauce, sugar and juice in a small bowl.

2 Place 1 sheet of rice paper in a medium bowl of warm water until just softened; lift sheet carefully from water and place on a clean tea-towel-covered board with a corner pointing towards you.

3 Place 1 level tablespoon of the vegetable mixture horizontally in centre of sheet; top with 1 mint leaf. Fold corner facing you over filling; roll rice paper to enclose filling, folding in sides.

4 Repeat with remaining rice paper sheets, vegetable mixture and mint leaves.

nutritional count per roll
▶ 0.2g total fat
▶ 0g saturated fat
▶ 100kJ (24 cal)
▶ 4.3g carbohydrate
▶ 0.9g protein
▶ 0.8g fibre

 GLUTEN FREE
 WHEAT FREE
DAIRY FREE
EGG FREE
 NUT FREE

test kitchen tip

Sushi is best made on
the day of serving.

nutritional count per sushi
- ► 0.6g total fat
- ► 0.1g saturated fat
- ► 339kJ (81 cal)
- ► 14.1g carbohydrate
- ► 4g protein
- ► 0.8g fibre

chicken teriyaki brown rice sushi

PREP + COOK TIME 1½ HOURS (+ STANDING & COOLING) **MAKES** 12

1 cup (200g) brown short-grain rice

2 cups (500ml) water

1 tablespoon rice vinegar

3 sheets toasted nori (yaki-nori)

1 lebanese cucumber (130g), seeded, cut into matchsticks

20g (¾ ounce) snow pea sprouts

2 tablespoons salt-reduced soy sauce

SUSHI VINEGAR

1 tablespoon rice vinegar

2 teaspoons white (granulated) sugar

¼ teaspoon fine salt

CHICKEN TERIYAKI

120g (4 ounces) chicken breast fillet, sliced thinly

1 tablespoon teriyaki sauce

1 clove garlic, crushed

1 Wash rice repeatedly in a large bowl with cold water until water is almost clear. Stand rice in a strainer for at least 30 minutes.

2 Make sushi vinegar. Make chicken teriyaki.

3 Place rice and the water in a medium saucepan, cover tightly; bring to the boil. Reduce heat; simmer, covered, about 30 minutes or until water is absorbed. Remove from heat; stand, covered, 10 minutes.

4 Spread rice into a large, non-metallic, flat-bottomed bowl (a wooden bowl is good for this). Using a plastic spatula, repeatedly slice through the rice at a sharp angle to break up the lumps and separate the grains, gradually pouring in sushi vinegar at the same time.

5 Continue to slice and turn the rice while fanning the rice with the other hand for about 5 minutes or until it is almost cool. Cover rice with a damp cloth to stop it drying out while making sushi.

6 Add rice vinegar to a medium bowl of cold water. Place one nori sheet, shiny-side down, lengthways across a bamboo mat about 2cm (¾ inch) from the edge of the mat closest to you. Dip fingers of one hand into the bowl of vinegared water, shake off excess; pick up one-third of the rice, place across centre of nori sheet.

7 Wet fingers again, then, working from left to right, gently rake rice evenly over nori, leaving 2cm (¾-inch) strip on the far side of the nori uncovered. Build up rice in front of the uncovered strip to form a mound to keep filling in place.

8 Place one-third of the cucumber, sprouts and chicken in a row across centre of rice, making sure the filling extends to both ends of the rice.

9 Starting with the edge closest to you, pick up mat using thumb and index fingers of both hands; use remaining fingers to hold filling in place as you roll mat away from you. Roll forward, pressing gently but tightly, wrapping nori around rice and filling.

10 Working quickly, repeat process to make a total of three rolls. Cut each roll into four pieces; trim ends. Serve with sauce.

SUSHI VINEGAR
Combine ingredients in a small jug.

CHICKEN TERIYAKI
Combine ingredients in a small bowl. Cook chicken mixture in a heated oiled small frying pan, over high heat, stirring, until cooked through; cool.

test kitchen tips

If you have a juice extractor, you
can use it to make the pineapple
and mango juice.
A mouli is a stainless steel utensil
used for grating or pureeing.

pine-orange and mango ice-blocks

PREP TIME 20 MINUTES (+ FREEZING) **MAKES** 8

1 medium pineapple (1.25kg), chopped coarsely

1 small mango (300g), chopped coarsely

½ cup (125ml) orange juice

1 Blend or process the pineapple and mango until smooth. Using a wooden spoon, push the mixture through a fine sieve or mouli into a large bowl. Stir in the juice.
2 Pour the mixture into 8 x ⅓-cup (80ml) ice-block moulds. Freeze for 3 hours or until firm.

guacamole and ham wrap

PREP TIME 15 MINUTES **MAKES** 4

2 avocados (500g)

1 tablespoon lime juice

1 small tomato (90g), seeded, chopped finely

130g (4 ounces) canned corn kernels, rinsed, drained

1 tablespoon finely chopped fresh chives

200g (6½ ounces) shaved ham

4 pieces dairy-free, egg-free, nut-free, lavash bread (240g)

1 Roughly mash avocado. Combine avocado and juice in a small bowl. Stir in tomato, corn and chives.
2 Spread each piece of bread with guacamole; top with ham. Roll bread tightly to enclose filling.

photograph page 56

---

nutritional count per ice-block
- ▶ 0.2g total fat
- ▶ 11g carbohydrate
- ▶ 0g saturated fat
- ▶ 1.2g protein
- ▶ 214kJ (51 cal)
- ▶ 2.1g fibre

nutritional count per wrap
- ▶ 23.2g total fat
- ▶ 40.1g carbohydrate
- ▶ 5.2g saturated fat
- ▶ 17.9g protein
- ▶ 1877kJ (449 cal)
- ▶ 4.7g fibre

test kitchen tip

The filling can be refrigerated
for up to two days.

guacamole and ham wrap (recipe page 55)

vegetable cakes

PREP + COOK TIME 25 MINUTES (+ COOLING) **MAKES** 4

1 tablespoon olive oil

¼ cup (60g) coarsely grated potato

2 tablespoons finely chopped red capsicum
(bell pepper)

2 tablespoons finely chopped
button mushrooms

2 eggs

1 Heat oil in a medium frying pan over medium heat; cook potato, stirring, for 5 minutes or until tender. Add capsicum and mushrooms; cook, stirring, for 3 minutes or until capsicum softens. Cool mixture for 10 minutes.

2 Combine the potato mixture with the eggs in a small bowl.

3 Place four oiled egg rings in a lightly oiled medium frying pan over low heat. Divide potato mixture between rings; flatten with a spatula or the back of a spoon. Cook, uncovered, for 5 minutes. Using an egg slide, turn rings; cook until vegetable cakes are browned lightly and set.

nutritional count per cake
▶ 7.4g total fat
▶ 1.4g saturated fat
▶ 368kJ (88 cal)
▶ 2.4g carbohydrate
▶ 3.8g protein
▶ 0.4g fibre

 GLUTEN FREE
 WHEAT FREE
 DAIRY FREE
NUT FREE

test kitchen tip

These vegetable cakes
are great cold for school
lunches or on a picnic.

test kitchen tip

Fritters can be stored in an
airtight container in the fridge
for up to 3 days. Eat cold or reheat
in a microwave oven on HIGH
(100%) for about 20 seconds.

indian vegetable fritters

PREP + COOK TIME 45 MINUTES **MAKES** 36

2 large carrots (360g), grated coarsely

1 large brown onion (200g), sliced thinly

2 cloves garlic, crushed

1 cup (120g) frozen peas

2 cups (300g) chickpea flour

1 teaspoon ground cumin

1 teaspoon garam masala

¼ teaspoon ground turmeric

½ teaspoon gluten-free baking powder

⅓ cup coarsely chopped coriander (cilantro)

¼ cup (60ml) water

vegetable oil, for deep-frying

1 Using hands, combine carrot, onion, garlic, peas, flour, spices, baking powder, coriander and the water in a medium bowl.

2 Heat oil in a wok or large saucepan to 180°C/350°F (or when a small cube of bread turns golden, about 15 seconds); deep-fry level tablespoons of vegetable mixture, in batches, until browned lightly and cooked through. Remove with a slotted spoon; drain on absorbent paper.

nutritional count per fritter
▶ 2g total fat
▶ 0.3g saturated fat
▶ 213kJ (51 cal)
▶ 5.8g carbohydrate
▶ 2.2g protein
▶ 1.6g fibre

GLUTEN FREE WHEAT FREE DAIRY FREE EGG FREE NUT FREE

minty lamb cutlets with mixed vegie smash

PREP + COOK TIME 40 MINUTES SERVES 4

1 tablespoon finely chopped fresh mint

⅓ cup (110g) mint jelly

2 teaspoons olive oil

1 teaspoon finely grated lemon rind

8 french-trimmed lamb cutlets (400g)

MIXED VEGIE SMASH

600g (1¼ pounds) baby new potatoes, halved

2 large carrots (360g), cut into 2cm (¾-inch) pieces

1 cup (120g) frozen peas

1 tablespoon olive oil

1 tablespoon lemon juice

2 tablespoons finely chopped fresh mint

1 Make mixed vegie smash.

2 Combine mint and jelly in a small bowl.

3 Rub combined oil and rind over lamb; cook lamb on a heated oiled grill plate (or grill or barbecue) over medium heat, for 3 minutes each side or until cooked as desired.

4 Serve lamb with smash and mint mixture.

MIXED VEGIE SMASH

Boil, steam or microwave potato, carrot and peas, separately, until tender; drain. Crush potato and peas roughly in a large bowl with a fork; stir in carrot and remaining ingredients.

nutritional count per serving
▸ 15.8g total fat
▸ 4.9g saturated fat
▸ 1572kJ (376 cal)
▸ 38.4g carbohydrate
▸ 16.3g protein
▸ 7.3g fibre

DAIRY FREE

EGG FREE

NUT FREE

test kitchen tip

If the mint jelly mixture
is a little too firm, stir in
about a tablespoon of
warm water.

test kitchen tip

You could serve this recipe with rice noodles or steamed rice instead of the hokkien noodles.

stir-fried beef with hokkien noodles

PREP + COOK TIME 30 MINUTES SERVES 4

450g (14½ ounces) thin hokkien noodles

1 tablespoon peanut oil

2 cloves garlic, crushed

600g (1¼ pounds) beef rump steak, sliced thinly

¼ cup (60ml) kecap manis

1 tablespoon fish sauce

1 tablespoon oyster sauce

1½ cups (120g) bean sprouts

100g (3 ounces) enoki mushrooms, trimmed

150g (4½ ounces) oyster mushrooms, chopped coarsely

4 green onions (scallions), sliced thickly

1 Place noodles in a medium heatproof bowl; cover with boiling water. Separate noodles with a fork, drain.

2 Heat oil in a wok; stir-fry garlic and beef, in batches, until beef is browned. Return beef mixture to wok with noodles, sauces, sprouts, mushrooms and onion; stir-fry until heated through. Serve with extra thinly sliced green onion, if you like.

nutritional count per serving
▶ 12.9g total fat
▶ 4.1g saturated fat
▶ 2387kJ (571 cal)
▶ 61.7g carbohydrate
▶ 47.6g protein
▶ 6g fibre

fish and oven-roasted chips

PREP + COOK TIME 55 MINUTES SERVES 4

5 small potatoes (600g)

1 teaspoon sea salt

½ teaspoon cracked black pepper

cooking-oil spray

4 x 120g (4-ounce) firm white fish fillets

2 tablespoons rinsed, drained baby capers

1 tablespoon finely chopped fresh dill

1 teaspoon finely grated lemon rind

⅓ cup (80ml) lemon juice

1 medium lemon (140g), cut into wedges

CITRUS SALAD

1 medium orange (240g)

1 lebanese cucumber (130g), chopped coarsely

40g (1½ ounces) baby spinach leaves

40g (1½ ounces) rocket leaves (arugula)

1 tablespoon white wine vinegar

1 Preheat oven to 220°C/425°F. Oil a large baking dish.

2 Cut each potato in half, then cut each half into six wedges. Combine potato, in a single layer, in baking dish with salt and pepper; spray lightly with cooking-oil. Roast about 45 minutes or until chips are browned lightly and tender.

3 Meanwhile, make citrus salad.

4 Cook fish in a heated oiled large frying pan, over medium heat, until browned both sides and cooked as desired.

5 Drizzle fish with combined capers, dill, rind and juice. Serve fish with chips, salad and wedges.

CITRUS SALAD

Peel and segment orange. Combine orange with remaining ingredients in a medium bowl.

GLUTEN FREE · WHEAT FREE · DAIRY FREE · EGG FREE · NUT FREE

nutritional count per serving
- ▶ 7g total fat
- ▶ 2.2g saturated fat
- ▶ 1141kJ (273 cal)
- ▶ 21.4g carbohydrate
- ▶ 27.7g protein
- ▶ 3.7g fibre

test kitchen tip

We used bream fillets in this recipe but you can use other firm white fish, such as whiting or john dory.

test kitchen tip

Strudel is best made just before
serving. You could replace the
apples with canned pears.

apple and sultana strudel

PREP + COOK TIME 40 MINUTES SERVES 8

2 tablespoons raw sugar

1 teaspoon ground cinnamon

2 sheets ready-rolled dairy-free puff pastry

400g (12½ ounces) canned pie apple

½ cup (80g) sultanas (golden raisins)

1 egg, beaten

1 Preheat oven to 200°C/400°F. Grease two oven trays.

2 Combine sugar and cinnamon in a small bowl.

3 Sprinkle 2 teaspoons of the sugar mixture over one pastry sheet. Place half the pie apple lengthways down one half of the pastry sheet; sprinkle with half the sultanas. Roll pastry carefully to enclose filling. Repeat process to make a second strudel.

4 Place strudels, seam-side down, on trays; brush with egg. Sprinkle strudels with remaining sugar mixture; bake, uncovered, for 20 minutes or until browned lightly. Stand 10 minutes before slicing.

nutritional count per serving
▶ 10.2g total fat
▶ 0.9g saturated fat
▶ 982kJ (235 cal)
▶ 32.1g carbohydrate
▶ 3.6g protein
▶ 1.7g fibre

passionfruit kisses

PREP + COOK TIME 40 MINUTES (+ COOLING) MAKES 24

3 eggs

½ cup (110g) caster (superfine) sugar

¾ cup (110g) (100% corn) cornflour (cornstarch)

2 tablespoons pure icing (confectioners') sugar

PASSIONFRUIT FILLING

90g (3 ounces) dairy-free spread

1½ cups (240g) pure icing (confectioners') sugar

2 tablespoons passionfruit pulp

1 Preheat oven to 180°C/350°F. Grease four 12-hole (1 tablespoon/20ml) shallow round-based patty pans.
2 Beat eggs in a small bowl with an electric mixer until thick and creamy. Add sugar, one tablespoon at a time, beating until sugar dissolves between additions. Gently fold in triple-sifted cornflour. Drop one level tablespoon of mixture into each pan hole.
3 Bake cakes for 10 minutes or until just cooked through. Turn cakes immediately onto a baking-paper-covered wire rack by tapping upside-down pans firmly on the bench to release the cakes; cool.
4 Meanwhile, make passionfruit filling.
5 Sandwich cold kisses with passionfruit filling; serve dusted with sifted pure icing sugar.

PASSIONFRUIT FILLING

Beat spread in a small bowl with an electric mixer until as white as possible; gradually beat in sifted icing sugar. Stir in passionfruit.

GLUTEN FREE WHEAT FREE DAIRY FREE NUT FREE

70

test kitchen tip

Kisses can be stored in an
airtight container for 1 day.
Unfilled kisses can be
frozen for up to 3 months.

nutritional count per kiss

▶ 3.7g total fat

▶ 0.7g saturated fat

▶ 485kJ (116 cal)

▶ 19.5g carbohydrate

▶ 0.9g protein

▶ 0.3g fibre

test kitchen tip

These biscuits will keep, stored in an airtight container at a cool room temperature, for at least a month.

apple and almond biscuits

PREP + COOK TIME 1¼ HOURS (+ COOLING) **MAKES** 40

3 egg whites

⅓ cup (75g) caster (superfine) sugar

¾ cup (110g) plain (all-purpose) flour

¼ teaspoon ground cinnamon

⅔ cup (110g) whole blanched almonds

1 cup (55g) finely chopped dried apples

1 Preheat oven to 180°C/350°F. Grease an 8cm x 26cm (3¼-inch x 10½-inch) bar cake pan; line base and long sides with baking paper, extending paper 5cm (2 inches) over sides.

2 Beat egg whites and sugar in a small bowl with an electric mixer until sugar dissolves. Fold in sifted flour then cinnamon, nuts and apple; spread mixture into pan.

3 Bake about 30 minutes. Stand in pan for 10 minutes before turning, top-side up, onto a wire rack to cool.

4 Reduce oven temperature to 150°C/300°F.

5 Using a serrated knife, cut into thin slices; place slices on oven trays. Bake for 15 minutes or until crisp. Turn onto a wire rack to cool.

nutritional count per biscuit
▶ 1.6g total fat
▶ 0.1g saturated fat
▶ 159kJ (38 cal)
▶ 4.8g carbohydrate
▶ 1.1g protein
▶ 0.5g fibre

DAIRY FREE

watermelon and strawberry ice-blocks

PREP + COOK TIME 15 MINUTES (+ REFRIGERATION & FREEZING) **MAKES** 4

⅓ cup (80ml) water

2 tablespoons white (granulated) sugar

350g (11 ounces) watermelon, seeded, chopped coarsely

80g (2½ ounces) strawberries, hulled, chopped coarsely

2 teaspoons lemon juice

1 Combine the water and sugar in a small saucepan; stir over low heat until sugar dissolves. Bring to the boil; boil, uncovered, without stirring, for 2 minutes or until mixture thickens slightly. Transfer syrup to a small bowl; refrigerate until cold.

2 Blend or process cold syrup with watermelon, strawberries and lemon juice until smooth. Pour mixture into four ⅓-cup (80ml) ice-block moulds. Freeze ice-blocks until firm, stirring occasionally during freezing to stop mixture from separating.

nutritional count per ice-block
- ▶ 0.2g total fat
- ▶ 0g saturated fat
- ▶ 238kJ (57 cal)
- ▶ 12.7g carbohydrate
- ▶ 0.5g protein
- ▶ 0.8g fibre

 GLUTEN FREE WHEAT FREE DAIRY FREE EGG FREE NUT FREE

Making desserts and baking without eggs might sound like a challenge. But, as you'll see from the recipes in this chapter, there's a delicious range of egg-free goodies that your children will love.

pork and cabbage salad

PREP TIME 20 MINUTES **SERVES** 1

1 small carrot (70g)

1 green onion (scallion), sliced thinly

60g (2 ounces) wombok (napa cabbage), shredded finely

60g (2 ounces) red cabbage, shredded finely

70g (2½ ounces) roast pork, shredded finely

DRESSING

1 tablespoon olive oil

2 teaspoons apple cider vinegar

½ teaspoon dijon mustard

1 Make dressing.
2 Using a vegetable peeler, slice carrot lengthways into thin ribbons.
3 Combine carrot, onion, wombok, red cabbage and pork in a bowl. Serve with dressing.

DRESSING
Place ingredients in a screw-top jar; shake well.

nutritional count per serving
▶ 21.2g total fat
▶ 3.6g saturated fat
▶ 1436kJ (342 cal)
▶ 8.8g carbohydrate
▶ 26.2g protein
▶ 6.9g fibre

 GLUTEN FREE WHEAT FREE DAIRY FREE EGG FREE NUT FREE

test kitchen tip

If you don't have any left-over
roast pork, it is also available,
in slices, from most delis.
Barbecued chicken or ham would
also work well in this recipe.

test kitchen tip

You could serve the
porridge with a dollop of
your favourite yoghurt.

porridge with pear compote

PREP + COOK TIME 20 MINUTES SERVES 4

3½ cups (875ml) hot water

1½ cups (135g) rolled oats

½ cup (125ml) milk

1 small pear (180g)

2 tablespoons blueberries

1 Combine the hot water and oats in a medium saucepan over medium heat; cook, stirring, for 5 minutes or until porridge is thick and creamy. Stir in milk.

2 Meanwhile, peel, core and coarsely chop pear. Place pear and ½ cup water into a small saucepan; bring to the boil. Reduce heat, simmer, uncovered, 5 minutes or until pear is soft.

3 Serve porridge topped with pear and drizzled with 1 tablespoon of the poaching liquid; sprinkle with berries.

nutritional count per serving
▶ 4.2g total fat
▶ 1.3g saturated fat
▶ 702kJ (168 cal)
▶ 25.7g carbohydrate
▶ 4.9g protein
▶ 4g fibre

strawberry soy smoothie (recipe page 84)

test kitchen tip

Always check the labels of soy products carefully for any unexpected allergens. You could substitute soy milk for rice milk, if you like.

strawberry soy smoothie

PREP TIME 10 MINUTES MAKES 1 CUP (250ML)

8 strawberries (160g), hulled, halved

½ cup (125ml) egg-free vanilla soy ice-cream (see test kitchen tip, page 83)

½ cup (125ml) chilled soy milk

1 Blend or process ingredients until smooth.
2 Pour into a glass; serve immediately.

photograph page 83

bran and cranberry muesli

PREP TIME 10 MINUTES SERVES 6

1 cup (90g) rolled oats

¾ cup (55g) all-bran

¼ cup (35g) dried cranberries

2 cups (500ml) milk

1 large banana (230g), sliced thinly

125g (4 ounces) fresh raspberries

1 Place oats, bran and cranberries in a small bowl; stir to combine.
2 To serve, place ⅓ cup muesli in each bowl; pour over ⅓ cup milk. Serve with bananas and raspberries.

---

nutritional count per 1 cup (250ml)

▶ 2.1g total fat ▶ 28.3g carbohydrate
▶ 0.4g saturated fat ▶ 7.6g protein
▶ 723kJ (173 cal) ▶ 6.2g fibre

nutritional count per serving

▶ 7.5g total fat ▶ 44.1g carbohydrate
▶ 0.9g saturated fat ▶ 8.3g protein
▶ 1162kJ (278 cal) ▶ 7.1g fibre

bran and cranberry muesli

test kitchen tips

Instead of using the dried
cranberries, use sultanas
or raisins.
To make this dairy-free,
use your preferred milk
in this recipe.

test kitchen tip

You can substitute the
extra ricotta with cream
cheese, if you like.

tuna and carrot pinwheels

PREP TIME 20 MINUTES MAKES 12

185g (6 ounces) canned tuna in brine, drained

1 small carrot (70g), chopped finely

2 gherkins (40g), chopped finely

2 tablespoons ricotta cheese

6 pieces egg-free, nut-free lavash bread (360g)

2 tablespoons ricotta cheese, extra

1 Combine tuna, carrot, gherkins and ricotta in a medium bowl.

2 Spread one piece of bread with a third of the extra ricotta; top with another piece of bread. Spread a third of the tuna mixture along one short edge of the bread. Roll bread tightly; trim edges.

3 Using a serrated knife, cut roll into four pieces. Repeat process to make a total of 12 pinwheels.

nutritional count per pinwheel
▶ 1.7g total fat
▶ 0.7g saturated fat
▶ 452kJ (108 cal)
▶ 17g carbohydrate
▶ 6g protein
▶ 1.3g fibre

EGG FREE   NUT FREE

teriyaki chicken rice paper rolls

PREP + COOK TIME 40 MINUTES (+ REFRIGERATION) MAKES 24

6 chicken thigh fillets (660g)

¼ cup (60ml) thick teriyaki marinade

2 tablespoons water

2 lebanese cucumbers (260g)

2 teaspoons peanut oil

24 x 17cm (6¾-inch) square rice paper sheets

200g (6½ ounces) enoki mushrooms, trimmed

test kitchen tip

Rolls can be made a day ahead; keep, covered with a damp paper towel, in the refrigerator.

1 Trim chicken; cut lengthways into eight strips. Combine chicken, marinade and the water in a small bowl, cover; refrigerate 1 hour. Drain chicken; discard marinade.

2 Meanwhile, cut cucumbers in half lengthways; discard seeds. Cut halves in half crossways; cut pieces into three strips lengthways.

3 Heat oil in a large frying pan over medium-high heat; cook chicken, in batches, until cooked through. Cool 10 minutes.

4 Place 1 sheet of rice paper in a medium bowl of warm water until just softened; lift sheet carefully from water, placing it on a clean tea-towel-covered board with a corner pointing towards you. Place two pieces of chicken horizontally in centre of rice paper; top with one piece of cucumber then a few mushrooms. Fold the corner facing you over filling; roll rice paper to enclose filling, folding in one side after first complete turn of roll. Repeat process to make a total of 24 rolls.

EGG FREE DAIRY FREE

nutritional count per roll
▶ 2.9g total fat
▶ 0.8g saturated fat
▶ 300kJ (72 cal)
▶ 5.4g carbohydrate
▶ 6g protein
▶ 0.2g fibre

antipasto melts

PREP + COOK TIME 10 MINUTES MAKES 2

2 small egg-free nut-free pizza bases (140g)

2 tablespoons sun-dried tomato pesto

8 artichoke quarters (200g)

60g (2 ounces) char-grilled capsicum
(bell pepper), sliced thinly

½ cup (50g) coarsely grated mozzarella cheese

1 Preheat grill (broiler).

2 Spread pizza bases with pesto; top with artichokes, capsicum and cheese.

3 Place under grill for 5 minutes or until cheese melts.

test kitchen tip

Add some chopped tomato
or mushrooms, if you like.

nutritional count per melt
▶ 10.8g total fat
▶ 4.1g saturated fat
▶ 1367kJ (327 cal)
▶ 38.7g carbohydrate
▶ 15.2g protein
▶ 6.8g fibre

EGG FREE

NUT FREE

bean nachos

PREP + COOK TIME 25 MINUTES SERVES 4

420g (13½ ounces) canned kidney beans, rinsed, drained

375g (12 ounces) mild thick and chunky tomato salsa

½ cup (125ml) water

230g (7 ounces) corn chips

2 cups (240g) coarsely grated cheddar cheese

1 small avocado (200g), mashed

⅔ cup (160g) sour cream

1 Preheat grill (broiler).

2 Place beans, salsa and the water in a medium frying pan over high heat; bring to the boil, simmer, uncovered, for 8 minutes or until mixture is thick.

3 Meanwhile, place corn chips in four ovenproof dishes; sprinkle with cheese. Place dishes on oven tray under the grill for 5 minutes or until cheese has melted.

4 Spoon bean mixture over hot corn chips; top with avocado. Accompany nachos with sour cream.

nutritional count per serving
▶ 39g total fat
▶ 18.4g saturated fat
▶ 2529kJ (605 cal)
▶ 47.7g carbohydrate
▶ 11.4g protein
▶ 10.2g fibre

EGG FREE   NUT FREE

test kitchen tip
**To make this gluten-free,
use gluten-free corn chips.**

test kitchen tip

Dried cranberries can be
replaced with sultanas or
chopped dates, if you like.

cranberry, oatmeal and cinnamon scones

PREP + COOK TIME 35 MINUTES MAKES 12

1 cup (160g) wholemeal self-raising flour

1 cup (150g) self-raising flour

½ cup (70g) fine oatmeal

1 teaspoon ground cinnamon

½ teaspoon finely grated lemon rind

30g (1 ounce) butter

¾ cup (105g) dried cranberries

1 cup (250ml) milk

2 tablespoons honey

1 tablespoon milk, extra

1 tablespoon fine oatmeal, extra

1 Preheat oven to 220°C/425°F. Grease and flour a deep 19cm (7¾-inch) square cake pan.

2 Combine flours, oatmeal, cinnamon and rind in a large bowl; rub in butter until mixture resembles breadcrumbs. Stir in cranberries, milk and honey.

3 Gently knead dough on a lightly floured surface until just smooth. Press dough into a 2cm (¾-inch) thickness. Cut 12 x 5.5cm (2¼-inch) rounds from dough; place in pan. Brush with extra milk then sprinkle with extra oatmeal. Bake for 25 minutes or until tops of scones sound hollow when tapped.

4 Serve scones warm with ricotta cheese and honey, if you like.

nutritional count per scone
▶ 6.1g total fat
▶ 3.5g saturated fat
▶ 836kJ (200 cal)
▶ 27.6g carbohydrate
▶ 7g protein
▶ 3.5g fibre

chicken, lentil and spinach pasta

PREP + COOK TIME 35 MINUTES SERVES 4

2 teaspoons olive oil

1 small brown onion (80g), chopped finely

2 cloves garlic, crushed

150g (4½ ounces) minced (ground) chicken

½ cup (100g) red lentils

2½ cups (625ml) chicken stock

¾ cup (180ml) water

¼ cup tomato paste (70g)

250g (8 ounces) baby spinach leaves

300g (9½ ounces) egg-free spiral pasta

1 Heat oil in a medium saucepan over medium heat; cook onion and garlic, stirring, for 5 minutes or until onion softens.

2 Add chicken; cook, stirring, for 5 minutes or until browned lightly. Stir in lentils, stock, the water and paste; bring to the boil. Reduce heat; simmer, uncovered, about 10 minutes or until lentils are tender. Add spinach; stir until wilted.

3 Meanwhile, cook pasta in a large saucepan of boiling water until just tender; drain.

4 Combine pasta and chicken mixture in a large bowl.

nutritional count per serving
▶ 7.6g total fat
▶ 1.7g saturated fat
▶ 1623kJ (388 cal)
▶ 59.1g carbohydrate
▶ 20g protein
▶ 5.3g fibre

DAIRY FREE

EGG FREE

NUT FREE

test kitchen tip

To make this gluten-free,
use gluten-free chicken
stock and pasta.

test kitchen tip

Many varieties of cooked
white beans are available
canned, among them
cannellini, butter and
haricot, all of which are
suitable for this recipe.

minestrone

PREP + COOK TIME 35 MINUTES SERVES 6

1 tablespoon olive oil

1 large brown onion (200g), chopped finely

2 cloves garlic, crushed

1 large carrot (180g), chopped finely

2 stalks celery (200g), trimmed, chopped finely

2 tablespoons tomato paste

2 cups (500ml) chicken stock

400g (12½ ounces) canned crushed tomatoes

1½ cups (375ml) water

425g (13½ ounces) canned white beans, rinsed, drained

½ cup (180g) small egg-free pasta shells

2 tablespoons fresh oregano leaves

1 Heat oil in a large saucepan over high heat; cook onion and garlic, stirring, for 5 minutes or until onion softens. Add carrot and celery; cook, stirring, for 5 minutes or until vegetables are tender. Add paste; cook, stirring, for 2 minutes.

2 Add stock, tomatoes and the water to the pan; bring to the boil. Add beans and pasta, reduce heat; simmer, uncovered, for 15 minutes or until pasta is cooked. Serve soup sprinkled with oregano.

nutritional count per serving
▶ 3.8g total fat
▶ 0.6g saturated fat
▶ 794kJ (190 cal)
▶ 29.4g carbohydrate
▶ 7g protein
▶ 4.9g fibre

DAIRY FREE   EGG FREE   NUT FREE

shepherd's pie

PREP + COOK TIME 1¼ HOURS MAKES 4

20g (¾ ounce) butter

1 small brown onion (80g), chopped finely

1 small carrot (70g), chopped finely

¼ teaspoon dried mixed herbs

2 cups (375g) finely chopped cooked lamb

2 tablespoons tomato paste

1 tablespoon tomato sauce (ketchup)

1 tablespoon worcestershire sauce

1 cup (250ml) beef stock

1 tablespoon plain (all-purpose) flour

2 tablespoons water

POTATO TOPPING

2 large potatoes (600g), chopped coarsely

40g (1½ ounces) butter

2 tablespoons warm milk

1 Preheat oven to 200°C/400°F. Spray four 1-cup (250ml) ovenproof dishes with cooking oil; place on an oven tray.

2 Make potato topping.

3 Meanwhile, melt butter in a medium saucepan over medium heat. Add onion and carrot; cook, stirring, for 5 minutes or until soft. Add herbs and lamb; stir for 2 minutes. Add paste, sauces and stock; stir until combined. Add combined flour and the water to pan; stir until mixture boils and thickens. Spoon lamb mixture into ovenproof dishes.

4 Spoon potato topping over lamb. Bake pies for 20 minutes or until topping is browned and pie is heated through. Stand 5 minutes before serving.

POTATO TOPPING

Boil, steam or microwave potato until tender; drain. Mash potato in a large bowl; stir in butter and warm milk, mash until smooth.

nutritional count per serving
▶ 24.7g total fat
▶ 8.4g saturated fat
▶ 1824kJ (436 cal)
▶ 12.5g carbohydrate
▶ 40.6g protein
▶ 6.5g fibre

test kitchen tip

This is a great way to use up leftovers from a roast lamb dinner. If you don't have leftover roast lamb, use 375g (12 ounces) of ground (minced) lamb instead: add it to the carrot and onion mixture in step 3, and cook, stirring with a wooden spoon, breaking up any large lumps, until the lamb is browned.

test kitchen tip

For an economical meal,
you can substitute the lamb
cutlets with lamb loin chops
or pork, beef or chicken.

lamb cutlets with ratatouille

PREP + COOK TIME 45 MINUTES SERVES 4

2 tablespoons olive oil

1 medium red onion (170g), sliced thinly

2 cloves garlic, crushed

1 large red capsicum (bell pepper) (350g), chopped coarsely

3 large zucchini (450g), halved lengthways, sliced thickly

5 baby eggplants (300g), sliced thickly

400g (12½ ounces) canned diced tomatoes

1 tablespoon tomato paste

12 french-trimmed lamb cutlets (900g)

1 Heat oil in a large saucepan over medium heat; cook onion, garlic, capsicum, zucchini and eggplant, stirring, for 5 minutes. Add tomatoes and paste; bring to the boil. Reduce heat; simmer, covered, about 20 minutes or until vegetables have softened.

2 Meanwhile, cook cutlets on a heated oiled grill plate (or grill or barbecue) 4 minutes each side or until cooked as desired. Serve with ratatouille.

nutritional count per serving
▶ 24.7g total fat
▶ 8.4g saturated fat
▶ 1824kJ (436 cal)
▶ 12.5g carbohydrate
▶ 40.6g protein
▶ 6.5g fibre

GLUTEN FREE WHEAT FREE DAIRY FREE EGG FREE NUT FREE

apple and berry crumble

PREP + COOK TIME 40 MINUTES SERVES 6

800g (1½ pounds) canned pie apple

2 cups (300g) frozen mixed berries

1 tablespoon white (granulated) sugar

½ cup (125ml) water

1 cup (120g) toasted muesli

2 tablespoons plain (all-purpose) flour

1 tablespoon light brown sugar

50g (1½ ounces) butter

½ cup (20g) corn flakes

1 Preheat oven to 180°C/350°F.

2 Combine apple, berries, white sugar and the water in a medium saucepan over high heat; bring to the boil. Reduce heat; simmer, stirring, until mixture is combined. Remove from heat.

3 Meanwhile, combine muesli, flour and brown sugar in a medium bowl. Using fingertips, rub in butter until mixture looks like coarse breadcrumbs; stir in cornflakes.

4 Place apple mixture in a 2-litre (8-cup) ovenproof dish; sprinkle with muesli mixture. Bake 20 minutes or until browned lightly.

test kitchen tip

The apple and berry filling can be made a day ahead; store, covered, in the fridge.

nutritional count per serving
- ▶ 9.1g total fat
- ▶ 5.2g saturated fat
- ▶ 1079kJ (258 cal)
- ▶ 41.5g carbohydrate
- ▶ 3.4g protein
- ▶ 6.1g fibre

test kitchen tip

Substitute the pears with apples, if you like.

chocolate, pear and hazelnut parcels

PREP + COOK TIME 40 MINUTES MAKES 4

12 sheets fillo pastry

cooking-oil spray

2 medium pears (460g), peeled, cored, sliced thinly lengthways

1 tablespoon light brown sugar

1 tablespoon chocolate-hazelnut spread

1 Preheat oven to 200°C/400°F. Grease and line two oven trays.

2 Place three sheets of fillo on a board; cover remaining sheets with baking paper then a damp tea towel to prevent them drying out. Spray each sheet of uncovered pastry with cooking-oil spray. Place half of 1 sliced pear lengthways down centre of pastry; top with 1 teaspoon each of the sugar and the spread.

3 Fold in the two long sides of the pastry then roll from one narrow side to enclose the filling. Place parcel, seam-side down, on an oven tray. Repeat process to make a total of 4 parcels.

4 Spray parcels with cooking-oil spray. Bake for 10 minutes or until browned lightly. Dust with sifted icing sugar before serving, if you like.

nutritional count per parcel
▶ 7.5g total fat
▶ 1g saturated fat
▶ 1246kJ (298 cal)
▶ 50.5g carbohydrate
▶ 4.4g protein
▶ 4.3g fibre

EGG FREE

choc-mint squares

PREP + COOK TIME 35 MINUTES (+ REFRIGERATION) **MAKES** 20

2⅓ cups (350g) milk chocolate Melts

2 teaspoons vegetable oil

¼ cup (60ml) pouring cream

2 x 35g (1-ounce) peppermint crisp chocolate bars, chopped finely

test kitchen tips

If you like, create stencils by cutting out 20 shapes or letters from baking paper. Position the stencils on the slice and dust with sifted cocoa powder. Carefully remove stencils.
Cut the slice into squares using a hot dry knife.

1 Grease an 8cm x 25cm (3¼-inch x 10-inch) bar cake pan; line base and sides with baking paper.
2 Combine ⅔ cup of the chocolate Melts and half of the oil in a small heatproof bowl; place bowl over a small saucepan of simmering water (don't let the water touch the base of the bowl), stirring until chocolate melts. Using a metal spatula, spread the chocolate mixture over the base of the prepared pan. Refrigerate until set.
3 Place cream and 1 cup of the remaining chocolate in a small saucepan; stir over low heat until mixture is smooth; cool 5 minutes. Stir peppermint crisps into chocolate cream mixture. Using a metal spatula, spread the peppermint chocolate mixture over the set chocolate base; refrigerate for 20 minutes.
4 Place the remaining chocolate and remaining oil in a small heatproof bowl; place bowl over a small saucepan of simmering water (don't let the water touch the base of the bowl), stirring until chocolate melts. Using a metal spatula, spread the chocolate mixture smoothly over the set peppermint chocolate; refrigerate 1 hour or overnight.
5 Using a hot dry knife, cut the slice into 2.5cm (1-inch) squares.

EGG FREE

nutritional count per square
▶ 6.9g total fat
▶ 4.2g saturated fat
▶ 497kJ (119 cal)
▶ 13.4g carbohydrate
▶ 1.6g protein
▶ 0.2g fibre

test kitchen tip

These can be made a day ahead; store in an airtight container in the fridge.

white chocolate cups with frûche and strawberries

PREP TIME 35 MINUTES MAKES 24

24 x 2.5cm (1-inch) paper patty-pan cases

cooking-oil spray

1 cup (150g) white chocolate Melts

½ cup (140g) vanilla frûche (fromage frais)

4 large strawberries, hulled, chopped finely

1 Spray paper patty-pan cases lightly with cooking-oil spray.

2 Place chocolate in a small saucepan; stir over low heat until chocolate is smooth. Using a cleaned new small pastry brush, paint chocolate thickly inside each case. Place paper cases on a tray; refrigerate for 5 minutes or until the chocolate sets.

3 Brush cases with a second coat of chocolate; refrigerate for another 5 minutes. Peel away and discard paper cases.

4 Meanwhile, combine frûche and strawberries in a small bowl; place 1 level teaspoon of the strawberry mixture into each chocolate case.

nutritional count per piece
▸ 2.4g total fat
▸ 1.5g saturated fat
▸ 176kJ (42 cal)
▸ 4.3g carbohydrate
▸ 0.9g protein
▸ 0.1g fibre

COOKING TECHNIQUES

Washing leeks removes any grit. Cut in half lengthwise, stopping at the root. Fan the layers out and wash under fast-running cold water.

Preparing asparagus To snap the woody end off the asparagus, hold it close to the base and bend it until it snaps. Discard the woody end. Trim with a vegetable peeler.

Cutting cucumbers into ribbons will give thin, uniform slices. The best tool for this is a vegetable peeler. Applying more pressure on the peeler gives thicker ribbons.

To seed a cucumber, cut the cucumber in half lengthways; use a teaspoon to scrape the seeds out into a bowl without piercing the skin.

To seed a vanilla pod, cut it in half lengthwise with a sharp knife. Hold the pod and scrape the seeds out with the edge of the knife.

To remove corn from fresh cobs, trim one side of the corn cob so it lies flat. Use a large flat-bladed knife to cut down the cob, close to the core, to remove the kernels.

Shredding wombok is easy using a V-slicer – you simply slide the cabbage back and forth across the blade. The adjustable blade is very sharp, so watch your fingers.

Slicing shallots These are best sliced thinly using a small sharp knife. If using whole, keep the root intact.

To grate beetroot, use the course (large) holes of the grater. It's best to wear disposable gloves as the juice can stain your hands.

To segment an orange, cut off the top and bottom, then slice down the orange, removing the peel and white pith. Cut out the segments between each membrane.

Zesting citrus fruit A zester has very small, and very sharp, holes that cut the rind (the outermost layer of the fruit) into thin ribbons but leaves the bitter pith behind.

Chiffonade is a way of cutting green leaves into long, thin strips. Lay leaves flat on top of each other, then roll up tightly and cut into thin slices.

Shredding nori These dried seaweed sheets are used to wrap sushi and as a garnish. Stack the sheets and cut into thin strips with a sharp knife.

To toast coconut, stir constantly in a dry frying pan over low heat until golden brown; as soon as it browns, remove it from the pan to stop it from overbrowning or burning.

To use fresh thyme leaves, hold the top of the stem with one hand and run the fingers of the other hand down the stem to strip off the leaves.

Crush, grind or blend spices in a mortar and pestle. To crush peppercorns, place them in the mortar (bowl) and pound vigorously with the pestle.

GLOSSARY

ALMONDS

flaked paper-thin slices.

ground also called almond meal. Almonds are ground to a coarse flour texture. Some commercially ground almonds may contain traces of wheat, gluten, peanuts (ground nuts) and tree nuts.

slivered small pieces cut lengthways.

APPLE CIDER VINEGAR made from crushed fermented apples.

ARROWROOT a starch made from a rhizome of a Central American plant; used mostly as a thickener.

BACON RASHERS also called bacon slices. Made from pork side, cured and smoked.

BAKING POWDER a raising agent; consists of two parts cream of tartar to one part bicarbonate of soda. Gluten-free baking powder is made without cereals.

BICARBONATE OF SODA a leavening (raising) agent; also called baking or carb soda.

BUTTER for recipes that aren't dairy-free, we use salted butter; 125g is equal to one stick (4 ounces) of butter. Unsalted butter, often called 'sweet' butter, simply has no added salt. It is mainly used in baking.

BUTTERMILK originally the term given to the slightly sour liquid left after butter was churned from cream, today it is made similarly to yoghurt. Sold alongside fresh milk products in supermarkets; despite its name, it is low in fat.

CAPERS the grey-green buds of a warm climate shrub, sold either dried and salted, or pickled in a vinegar brine; tiny young ones, called baby capers, are also available both in brine or dried in salt. All capers must be rinsed before using.

CAPSICUM also known as pepper or bell pepper. They can be red, green, yellow, orange or purplish-black. Discard seeds and membranes before use.

char-grilled capsicum available in jars in brine or oil from supermarkets, or singularly from delicatessens.

CHEESE

cream commonly called Philadelphia or Philly; a soft cow's-milk cheese.

mascarpone a fresh cultured-cream product made similarly to yoghurt. White to creamy yellow in colour with a buttery-rich texture.

parmesan also known as parmigiano, a hard, grainy cow's-milk cheese that originated in the Parma region of Italy. The curd is salted in brine for a month before being aged for up to two years in humid conditions.

pizza a blend of grated mozzarella, cheddar and parmesan cheeses.

ricotta a sweet, moist, soft, white, cow's-milk cheese; has a slightly grainy texture.

CHOCOLATE

chocolate-hazelnut spread we use Nutella. Originally developed when chocolate was hard to source during World War 2, so hazelnuts were added to the chocolate supply.

dark (70% cocoa solids) also called semi-sweet; made with a high percentage of cocoa liquor and cocoa butter, and a little added sugar.

Melts small discs of compound milk, white or dark chocolate; is ideal for melting and moulding.

white contains no cocoa solids but derives its sweet flavour from cocoa butter. Is very sensitive to heat so watch carefully if melting.

COCOA POWDER dried, roasted, unsweetened and ground cocoa beans (cacao seeds).

COCONUT

desiccated concentrated, dried, unsweetened and finely shredded coconut flesh.

flaked dried flaked coconut flesh.

shredded thin strips of unsweetened dried coconut.

CORNED BEEF usually sold vacuum-sealed in brine. Made from topside roast, also known as silverside.

CORNFLAKES, GLUTEN-FREE available from health-food stores and some supermarkets.

CORNFLOUR also known as cornstarch; used as a thickening agent. Available as 100% corn (maize) and wheaten cornflour. If you have a gluten allergy, make sure you use 100% corn cornflour.

CREAM we use fresh pouring cream, also known as pure cream.

sour a thick, commercially-cultured sour cream with at least 35% fat content.

thickened a whipping cream containing a thickener. Has at least 35% fat content.

CREAM OF TARTAR acid ingredient in baking powder; also used in confectionery mixtures to help prevent sugar from crystallising.

CUMIN also known as zeera or comino; resembling caraway in size, cumin is the dried seed of a plant related to the parsley family having a spicy, nutty flavour. Available in seed form or dried and ground.

DAIRY-FREE SPREAD or dairy-free margarine, is a commercially-made margarine, free of dairy products. There are a number of dairy-free spreads available from supermarkets.

DIJON MUSTARD also known as french mustard. A pale brown, creamy, distinctively flavoured, fairly mild French-style mustard.

EGGS some recipes in this book may call for raw or barely cooked eggs; exercise caution if there is a salmonella problem in your area. The risk is greater for those who are pregnant, elderly or very young, and with impaired immune systems.

FISH FILLETS use any boneless firm white fish fillet – blue eye, bream swordfish, ling, whiting or sea perch are all good choices. Check for small bones and remove with tweezers.

FLOUR

bread mix, gluten-free a commercial gluten-free bread mix available from health-food stores and most major supermarkets.

buckwheat not a true cereal, but a flour is made from its seeds. Available from health-food stores.

chickpea also called besan or gram; made from ground chickpeas so is gluten-free and high in protein.

plain all-purpose flour made from wheat. It is also available in gluten-free form from health-food stores and most supermarkets.

potato made from cooked potatoes that have been dried and ground.

rice a very fine, almost powdery, gluten-free flour; most often made from ground white rice.

self-raising (rising) plain flour mixed with baking powder in the proportion of 1 cup flour to 2 teaspoons baking powder. Gluten-free is also available from health-food stores and most major supermarkets.

soy made from ground soya beans.

GARAM MASALA a blend of cardamom, cinnamon, cloves, coriander, fennel and cumin, roasted and ground together.

GELATINE we use powdered gelatine. It is also available in sheet form (leaf gelatine).

GLACÉ FRUIT (cherries, pineapple etc) when buying glacé fruit check the ingredients label for 'glucose made from wheat'; glacé fruit is available without glucose, making it gluten-free and wheat-free.

GOLDEN SYRUP a by-product of sugarcane.

HAZELNUTS also known as filberts; plump, grape-sized, rich, sweet nuts.
ground known as hazelnut meal.

JALAPEÑO (hah-lah-pain-yo) a fairly hot, medium-sized, dark green chilli; available pickled, sold canned or bottled, and fresh, from greengrocers.

JAM also known as preserve or conserve; usually made from fruit.

KUMARA the Polynesian name of an orange-fleshed sweet potato often confused with yam.

LAVASH flat, unleavened bread of Mediterranean origin.

LINSEED, SUNFLOWER AND ALMOND MEAL (LSA) available from health-food stores and most major supermarkets.

MAPLE SYRUP, PURE distilled from the sap of maple trees. Maple-flavoured syrup or pancake syrup is not an adequate substitute for the real thing.

MIXED PEEL candied citrus peel.

MUSHROOMS

button small, cultivated white mushrooms with a delicate, subtle flavour.

enoki also known as enokitake; grown and bought in clumps, these delicately-flavoured mushrooms have small cream caps on long thin stalks. Available from Asian food shops and most supermarkets.

oyster also known as abalone; grey-white mushroom shaped like a fan. Prized for their smooth texture and subtle, oyster-like flavour.

portobello mature swiss browns. Large, dark brown mushrooms with full-bodied flavour.

swiss brown (also called roman or cremini) are light-to-dark brown in colour with a full-bodied flavour. Place on a tray in a single layer, covered with damp absorbent paper, and store them in an area where cool air can circulate around them.

shiitake when fresh are also known as chinese black, forest or golden oak mushrooms; although cultivated, they have the earthiness and taste of wild mushrooms. Are large and meaty; often used as a substitute for meat in some vegetarian dishes. When dried, they are known as donko or dried chinese mushrooms; rehydrate before use.

NOODLES

hokkien also known as stir-fry noodles; fresh wheat noodles resembling thick, yellow-brown spaghetti needing no pre-cooking before being used.

rice, fresh soft white noodles made from rice flour and vegetable oil; available in varying thicknesses, from thin to broad and flat. Rinse under hot water to remove starch and excess oil before using.

rice vermicelli also called sen mee, mei fun or bee hoon; used in spring rolls and salads. Before using, soak dried noodles in hot water until softened, boil briefly then rinse with hot water.

OIL

cooking spray we use a cholesterol-free cooking spray made from canola oil.

olive made from ripened olives. Extra virgin and virgin are the best, while extra light or light refers to taste not fat levels.

peanut pressed from ground peanuts; most commonly used oil in Asian cooking because of its high smoke point (capacity to handle high heat without burning).

rice bran the oil is extracted from the germ and inner husk of the rice grain; has a mild, slightly nutty, flavour. Its high smoke point means it's suitable for high-temperature cooking methods such as stir-frying and deep-frying.

sesame made from roasted, crushed, white sesame seeds; a flavouring rather than a cooking medium.

vegetable sourced from plants.

OLIVES the colour of olives depends on their level of ripeness. Green olives are picked before fully ripened, while black olives are those picked when ripe. Green olives, generally, are denser, firmer and more bitter than black ones. Black olives have a richer and more mellow flavour and are softer in texture.

ONIONS

brown and white these onions are interchangeable, however, white onions have a more pungent flesh.

green also called scallions or, incorrectly, shallots; an immature onion picked before the bulb has formed, has a long, bright-green edible stalk.

red also called spanish, red spanish or bermuda onion; a large, purple-red, sweet-flavoured, onion.

PANCETTA
an Italian unsmoked bacon; pork belly is cured in salt and spices then rolled into a sausage shape and dried for several weeks.

PEPPERMINT CRISP
a chocolate bar with a crisp peppermint centre covered with chocolate.

POLENTA
also called cornmeal; a flour-like cereal made of corn (maize). Also the dish made from it.

PISTACHIOS
delicately flavoured green-coloured nuts inside hard off-white shells. Available salted or unsalted in their shells; you can also buy them shelled. We use shelled, unsalted nuts in our recipes.

RICE

rice paper sheets also known as banh trang. Made from rice paste and stamped into rounds; stores well at room temperature. They are quite brittle and will break if dropped; dipped momentarily in water they become pliable wrappers for fried and uncooked vegetables.

puffed rice that has been steamed and puffed; available in the health-food isle of supermarkets.

rolled flattened rice grain rolled into flakes; looks similar to rolled oats.

vinegar a colourless vinegar made from fermented rice and flavoured with sugar and salt. Also known as seasoned rice vinegar.

ROCKET
also known as arugula, rugula and rucola; a peppery-tasting green leaf used similarly to baby spinach leaves.

baby rocket leaves, also known as wild rocket, are smaller and less peppery than the mature leaf.

SALMON, SMOKED
fresh salmon that has been hot or cold-smoked. Available in the refrigerated section at supermarkets.

SAUCES

fish also called nam pla or nuoc nam; made from pulverised salted fermented fish, most often anchovies. Has a pungent smell and strong taste, so use sparingly.

kecap manis a dark, thick sweet soy sauce used in most South-East Asian cuisines. Depending on the brand, the soy's sweetness is from the addition of either molasses or palm sugar when brewed.

oyster Asian in origin, this rich, brown sauce is made from oysters and brine, cooked with salt and soy sauce, and thickened with starches.

soy also known as sieu, is made from fermented soya beans. Several variations are available in most supermarkets and Asian food stores. We use a mild Japanese variety in our recipes; possibly the best table soy and the one to choose if you only want one variety.

light soy a fairly thin, pale but salty tasting sauce, is used in dishes in which the natural colour of the ingredients is to be maintained. Do not confuse with salt-reduced or low-sodium soy sauces.

teriyaki usually made from soy sauce, mirin, sugar, ginger and other spices; it imparts a distinctive glaze when brushed on grilled meat.

tomato also known as ketchup or catsup; a flavoured condiment made from tomatoes, vinegar and spices.

worcestershire a dark coloured sauce made from garlic, soy sauce, onions, tamarind, molasses, lime, anchovies, vinegar and other seasonings.

SPINACH
also known as english spinach and, incorrectly, silver beet.

SUGAR

brown a soft, finely granulated sugar with molasses for its flavour.

caster also called superfine or finely granulated table sugar.

pure icing also known as powdered or confectioners' sugar. Pure icing sugar has no added cornflour, so tends to clump.

white a coarsely granulated table sugar, also called crystal sugar.

SUNFLOWER SEED KERNELS
small grey-green, slightly soft, oily kernels.

TURMERIC
also known as kamin, fresh turmeric must be grated or pounded to release its somewhat acrid aroma and pungent flavour.

TOMATO

cherry also known as tiny tim or tom thumb tomatoes, small and round.

egg also known as plum or roma tomatoes, these are smallish, oval-shaped tomatoes often used in Italian cooking or salads.

grape are about the size of a grape; they can be oblong, pear or grape-shaped and are often used whole in salads or eaten as a snack.

semi-dried partially dried tomato pieces in olive oil; softer and juicier than sun-dried, these are not a preserve so do not keep as long as sun-dried tomatoes.

VANILLA

bean dried, long, thin pod from a tropical golden orchid; the minuscule black seeds inside the bean are used to impart a luscious vanilla flavour.

extract vanilla beans are pulped into a mixture with alcohol and water. Only a couple of drops are needed.

WOMBOK
(napa cabbage) also called chinese or peking cabbage; elongated in shape with pale green, crinkly leaves, this is the most common cabbage in South-East Asia.

YOGHURT
we use plain full-cream yoghurt unless stated otherwise.

INDEX

Published in 2013 by Bauer Media Books

Bauer Media Books is a division of Bauer Media Limited

54 Park St, Sydney

GPO Box 4088, Sydney, NSW 2001.

phone (02) 9282 8618; fax (02) 9126 3702

www.awwcookbooks.com.au

MEDIA GROUP

BAUER MEDIA BOOKS

Publisher - Sally Wright

Editorial and Food Director - Pamela Clark

Sales & rights director Brian Cearnes

Creative Director - Hieu Chi Nguyen

Published and Distributed in the United Kingdom by Octopus Publishing Group

Endeavour House

189 Shaftesbury Avenue

London WC2H 8JY

United Kingdom

phone (+44)(0)207 632 5400; fax (+44)(0)207 632 5405

info@octopus-publishing.co.uk;

www.octopusbooks.co.uk

Printed by Toppan Printing Co., China

International foreign language rights, Brian Cearnes, Bauer Media Books bcearnes@bauer-media.com.au

A catalogue record for this book is available from the British Library.

ISBN: 978 174245 280 7 (pbk.)

© Bauer Media Ltd 2013

ABN 18 053 273 546

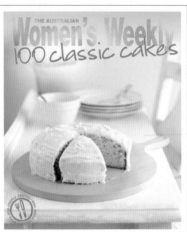

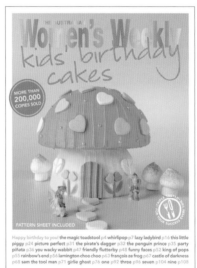